MILITARY MACHINES

DRONES

By Ryan Nagelhout

Gareth Stevens
Publishing

Please visit our website, www.garethstevens.com. For a free color catalog of all our high-quality books, call toll free 1-800-542-2595 or fax 1-877-542-2596.

Library of Congress Cataloging-in-Publication Data

Nagelhout, Ryan.
 Drones / Ryan Nagelhout.
    p. cm. — (Military machines)
 Includes index.
 ISBN 978-1-4339-8458-7 (pbk.)
 ISBN 978-1-4339-8459-4 (6-pack)
 ISBN 978-1-4339-8457-0 (library binding)
 1. Drone aircraft–Juvenile literature. I. Title.
 UG1242.D7N33 2013
 623.74'69—dc23

                                    2012020378

First Edition

Published in 2013 by
Gareth Stevens Publishing
111 East 14th Street, Suite 349
New York, NY 10003

Copyright © 2013 Gareth Stevens Publishing

Designer: Michael J. Flynn
Editor: Kristen Rajczak

Photo credits: Courtesy of the US Air Force: cover, p.1 by Staff Sgt. Brian Ferguson, 12, 18–19 by Tech. Sgt. Sabrina Johnson, 21 by Master Sergeant Steve Horton; pp. 4, 5 Ethan Miller/Getty Images; courtesy of the US Navy: pp. 6–7, 13, 17 by PH2 Carnes; pp. 8, 9 John Moore/Getty Images; p. 11 http://en.wikipedia.org/wiki/File:Cropped_RDenny.jpg; p. 15 http://en.wikipedia.org/wiki/File:Ryan_Model_147.jpg; courtesy of US Marine Corps: p. 16 by LCpl. E. J. Young; p. 20 http://en.wikipedia.org/wiki/File:MQ-9_Reaper_CBP.jpg; courtesy of US Army: pp. 23 by Kevin Goode, 24–25 by Sgt. 1st Class Michael Guillory; p. 27 Erik Simonsen/Photographer's Choice/Getty Images; pp. 28–29 by Victor Habbick Visions/Getty Images.

Printed in the United States of America

CPSIA compliance information: Batch #CW13GS: For further information contact Gareth Stevens, New York, New York at 1-800-542-2595.

CONTENTS

Words in the glossary appear in **bold** type the first time they are used in the text.

THE NEW COCKPIT

Two people sit wearing headsets in a room lit only by computers. Their screens show images and video of a city, taken from above. They watch fuel levels and other important **vehicle** features on another screen. Gripping joysticks and barking out commands, the two work side by side. Are they playing a video game? Running a test? Training to be pilots?

No, these are soldiers on the cutting edge of military machines. Operating a UAV, or unmanned **aerial** vehicle, these pilots are controlling a plane carrying out a **mission** thousands of miles away.

These airmen are flying a UAV from Creech Air Force Base in Nevada.

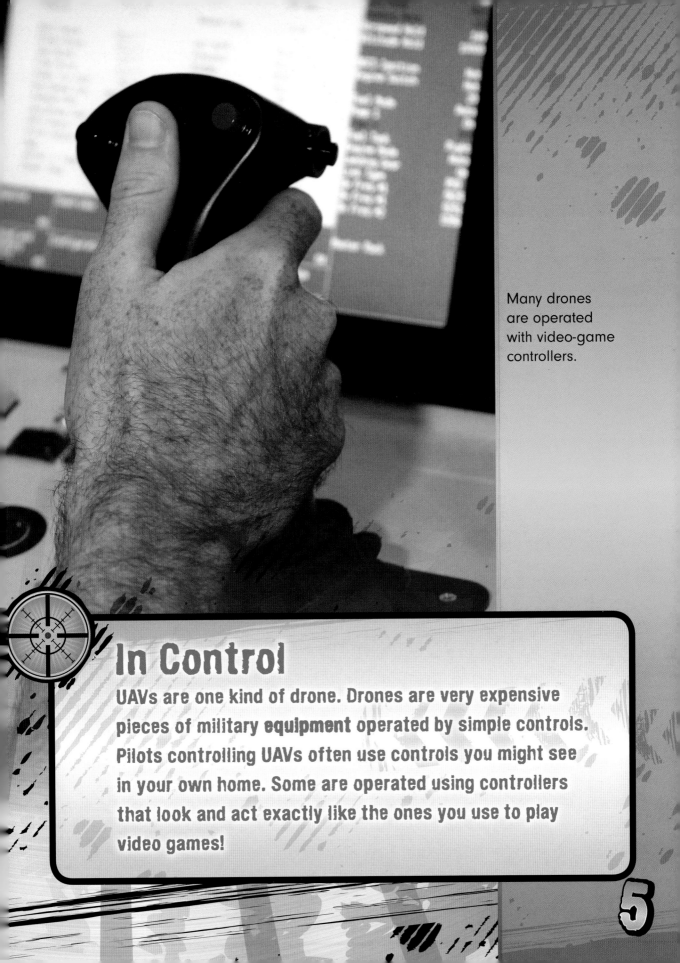

Many drones are operated with video-game controllers.

In Control

UAVs are one kind of drone. Drones are very expensive pieces of military equipment operated by simple controls. Pilots controlling UAVs often use controls you might see in your own home. Some are operated using controllers that look and act exactly like the ones you use to play video games!

Drones are the future of the military. From the US Air Force to the navy, each branch is working with this exciting **technology** like never before. Drones can serve a variety of purposes for the military. They help wage war while keeping soldiers out of harm's way.

Drones come in many shapes and sizes. Some drones have wheels and roll on the ground, while many fly like airplanes. There are even UAVs that fly like helicopters. All drones are unmanned, meaning something or someone else controls them in another location. Some drones are controlled thousands of miles away from where they are working.

The Pigeon

Greek mathematician and scientist Archytas invented the earliest self-flying machines around 400 BC. Archytas created a steam-powered pigeon made of wood, which hung on a wire and moved as steam escaped. The bird used a scientific idea that wasn't identified for centuries called the action-reaction principle.

Drones have
taken the place
of many pilots
in the US military.

THE THREE Ds

Drones can do jobs that humans can't or just don't want to do. Researchers call these the "Three Ds." The first D stands for "dull." Drones can do dull jobs, or things that may take longer than a person can work on the task.

The second D is for "dirty." Drones can handle unsafe materials and explore places humans can't go, such as deep underwater or high above Earth.

The third D is "dangerous." Drones can carry out tasks in order to keep humans safe. They can disarm bombs and carry out searches in unstable areas, such as caves.

The soldier pictured on the next page is using a remote to control this robot as it finds bombs on the side of the road.

Drones are used whenever possible to keep soldiers safe.

World War Wonders

Drones saw limited use in World War I, mostly on the German side. They had a wire-guided motorboat called the FL-7 that was created to crash into enemy ships and explode. In 1916, the Germans started using a radio-control system invented by Nikola Tesla to make the FL-7 more effective.

A HOLLYWOOD PRODUCTION

Reginald Denny was a British pilot during World War I who later became a movie star. While acting in Hollywood, Denny began to tinker with radio-controlled model airplanes used on movie sets. He made his own model planes and eventually began selling them in a hobby shop.

In 1938, Denny won a military contract—$30,000 to make RP-4 Radioplanes, or "Dennymites," for **antiaircraft** gun target practice. Denny's Radioplane company made nearly 15,000 of these drones for the US Army. The Dennymites had a wingspan of 12 feet 3 inches (3.7 m). They were the first mass-produced unmanned planes in history.

Stargazing

Denny's factory started more than just drone production. Norma Jeane Mortenson worked on the factory's assembly line. She was photographed there in 1945 and encouraged to pose for more pictures. Mortenson later changed her name to Marilyn Monroe and became one of the most famous actresses of the 1950s.

Reginald Denny paved the way for future unmanned aircraft.

APHRODITE AND ANVIL

The first time American forces used unmanned planes during combat came in World War II when the air force and navy created Operation Aphrodite, also known as Project Anvil. Planes too old for normal operation were loaded with explosives and flown using radio control into German targets, such as boats.

A pilot and copilot flew the plane to a certain height and then jumped out, using parachutes to land safely. Pilots on a "mother" plane then controlled the unmanned plane. They guided the plane to its target using cameras. Many problems limited the operation's successes, and the project ended in 1945.

Operation Aphrodite was generally seen as a failure, but it was the first major unmanned plane operation for the US military.

Many of the US Navy's PB4Y-2S Privateer planes, like the one pictured here, became outfitted for unmanned flights.

Drone Disaster

These first unmanned plane operations had many accidents, but one was especially deadly. In August 1944, a plane exploded in flight, killing two men before they could parachute to safety. The pilot, Joe Kennedy Jr., was the older brother of John F. Kennedy, who later became president of the United States.

FIRE AND LIGHTNING

After World War II, some air force officials were afraid drones could put pilots out of work. However, the Cold War created a unique need for drones that could conduct **surveillance**. After a U-2 spy plane was shot down in 1960, US military leaders wanted a way to monitor the enemy without losing pilots.

A top-secret program called Lightning Bug (later Fire Fly) **developed** drones for exactly this purpose. These **reconnaissance** drones also flew more than 3,000 missions in Southeast Asia from 1962 to 1975. They helped map the jungle and jam enemy radio signals during the Vietnam War.

The Cuban Missile Crisis

For 13 days in October 1962, the United States thought the Soviet Union had nuclear weapons in Cuba. Drones were ready to do surveillance over Cuba, but they weren't sent out. The US military didn't want the Soviets to discover its secret technology.

Drones carried out many surveillance missions during the Vietnam War.

15

GULF PIONEERS

Israel helped develop drone technology in the 1980s, including a drone called the Pioneer. Launched from ships or military bases, the Pioneer could fly for 115 miles (185 km) and was used by the United States in the 1991 Persian Gulf War.

An RQ-2A Pioneer UAV prepares to launch from the top of a truck.

During one mission in 1991, a Pioneer drone made a low pass over a group of enemy troops near Kuwait City, Kuwait. The soldiers waved white bed sheets and shirts at the drone as it went by, signaling **surrender**. It was the first time enemy soldiers ever surrendered to an unmanned aircraft. The drone now sits in the Smithsonian National Air and Space Museum in Washington, DC.

The materials used to make Pioneer drones and their small size made them hard for enemies to detect.

DARPA

The Defense Advanced Research Projects Agency, or DARPA, is the research arm of the United States Department of Defense. It has developed many drones, including the SolarEagle, a giant drone that can stay in the air for up to 5 years. It has also issued "grand challenges" to scientists to build self-driving cars and other robotics.

FLYING FORWARD

The start of the 21st century brought a boom in drone development. Smaller engines and better cameras helped drones become smarter and more useful for military operations.

The use of global positioning systems, or GPS, has also made it easier to control drones from far away. Pilots can program a location into a drone's GPS and let it locate and track possible military targets. GPS allows drones to fly to distant places with less direction and input from their operators.

The Predator drones were commonly used by the US military in Iraq and Afghanistan.

By 2000, weapons systems began to appear on drones invented for reconnaissance. These additions highlighted a new, more deadly purpose for the drones.

A New War

The **terrorist** attacks on September 11, 2001, brought the United States into a "war on terror" as it invaded Afghanistan and Iraq. The military, which once had only a few drones, had several thousand in use by 2012. Drones have also carried out surveillance and attacks in Iran, Pakistan, Yemen, Syria, Somalia, and Libya.

ON THE PROWL

Among the most successful drones for the military are the MQ-1 and RQ-1 Predator drones. First used in 1995 in missions over Bosnia, these UAVs have flown thousands of missions for the air force in the last two decades.

RQ-1 Predator drones were originally made for surveillance only. But in 2002, they began to be outfitted with weapons and used for targeted strikes as well. These MQ-1 Predators were the true beginning of unmanned warfare.

The US military started to phase out the Predator in favor of more advanced Reaper drones in 2011.

The Reaper is twice as fast and can carry 10 times as much weight as the Predator.

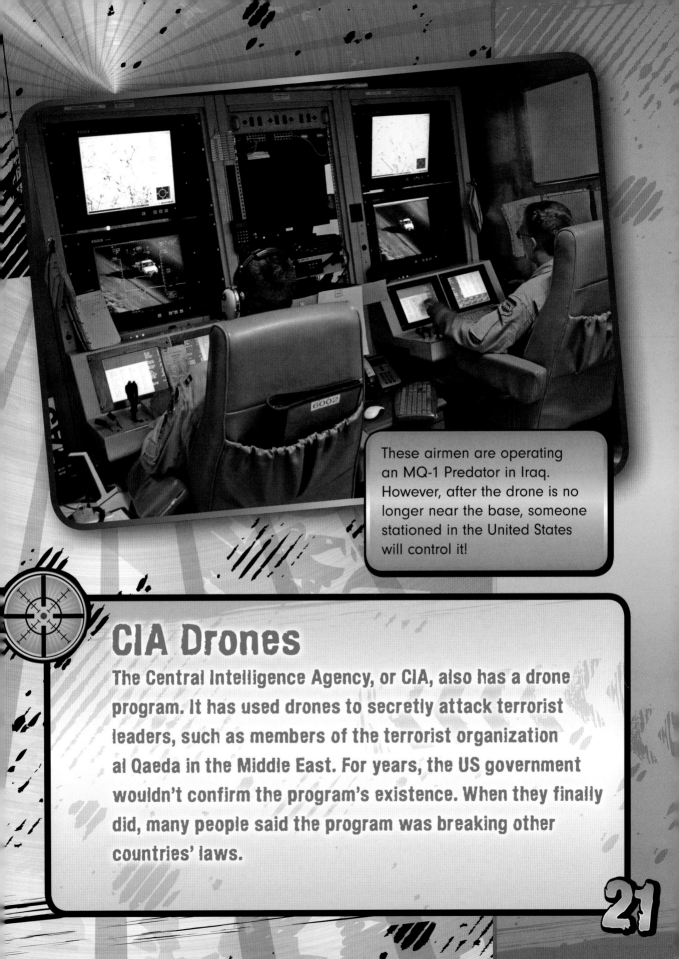

These airmen are operating an MQ-1 Predator in Iraq. However, after the drone is no longer near the base, someone stationed in the United States will control it!

CIA Drones

The Central Intelligence Agency, or CIA, also has a drone program. It has used drones to secretly attack terrorist leaders, such as members of the terrorist organization al Qaeda in the Middle East. For years, the US government wouldn't confirm the program's existence. When they finally did, many people said the program was breaking other countries' laws.

GROUND DRONES

Not all drones take to the skies. Unmanned ground vehicles, or UGVs, are used in combat to keep soldiers safe while on land. These vehicles are commonly controlled by a soldier close by, not with a **satellite** like flying drones sometimes are.

Robotics maker iRobot makes a number of drones that drive like tanks over rough ground. The 110 FirstLook is small and can be thrown over walls and other **obstacles** to explore dangerous areas. The vehicle can even right itself if it falls over. Other drones can be used to find bombs and stop them from blowing up, or to carry heavy equipment.

Robot Soccer

Some robots are developed for sport, not war. An organization called RoboCup has developed robots that play soccer! Soccer games help their researchers create robots that move better and quickly adapt to changes. Organizers say their goal is to make a team that can one day win the human World Cup.

Drones that find and stop improvised explosive devices, or IEDs, hidden in the ground save countless lives.

HAND AND SEA

Most aerial drones can take flight on their own, but smaller ones need a bit of human help. A single soldier can throw small, lightweight drones to help them take flight and carry out missions. Many of these can also be taken apart and easily moved for quick surveillance missions.

A soldier stationed in Iraq gets ready to launch a Raven UAV into the sky.

High-powered cameras, such as those on the Raven drone, can explore a large area much faster than could be done on the ground by humans. Raven drones look very similar to model airplanes and weigh just 5 pounds (2.3 kg).

Drones may take to the water soon, too. The navy is working on unmanned boats and submarines!

Hollywood Drones

As technology advances, drones have made a splash on the big screen as well. In 2004, *iRobot*, starring Will Smith, featured human-like robots and self-driving cars. In 2005, *Stealth* featured a supersmart drone jet that the military loses control of. Hollywood loves to cause trouble with robots!

THE FOURTH D

Scientists say drones operating **autonomously** could be more capable than human-run UAVs. This is because of the fourth D: dispassion, or lack of emotion. Drones may make better decisions because they're not affected by stress or other strains while on a mission. Where drone pilots can only work in 6- or 8-hour shifts, a self-operating drone can work endlessly under its own control.

Drones are also unaffected by what soldiers call the "fog of war," or the confusion that comes from being in a loud, scary combat situation. Using a dispassionate drone could prevent mistakes and accidents on the battlefield.

"A Man in the Loop"

Military officials say armed drones always have "a man in the loop," or a human making decisions. While not in active use by the military yet, the technology enabling drones to fly and land without a pilot already exists. As this continues to be tested, military leaders ask: Should drones be allowed to make their own decisions?

Armed drones
always have a
pilot in charge,
but someday that
could change.

DRONES OF THE FUTURE

Drone technology continues to advance as the military keeps putting time and money into its development. In 2012, one-third of all military aircraft were drones, a huge increase from the number in service a decade earlier.

New models can now land on aircraft carriers and take part in more involved missions. Researchers hope, as drones become smarter and more useful, they can find new ways to keep soldiers out of harm's way.

As more pilots sign up to fly drones instead of jets, the way we wage war continues to change. You never know who, or what, will be flying overhead next.

Drones at Home

Private companies and cities are beginning to use drones as well. Some universities do research with drones. Police departments in cities such as Seattle, Washington, and Houston, Texas, use them to patrol. Drones are used to watch the Mexican–American border. Even farmers can use drones to spray crops.

Advances in technology will let drones do more for our military than ever before.

GLOSSARY

aerial: operating in the air

antiaircraft: meant to guard against attacks from the air

autonomously: working on its own

develop: to create or produce by effort over time

equipment: tools and machines needed for an activity

mission: a task or job a group must perform

obstacle: something that stands in the way

reconnaissance: the exploration of a place to collect information

satellite: an object that circles Earth

surrender: to give up

surveillance: the act of watching someone or something closely

technology: the practical application of specialized knowledge

terrorist: one who uses violence and fear to challenge an authority

vehicle: an object used for carrying or transporting people or goods, such as a car, truck, or airplane

FOR MORE INFORMATION

Books

Hamilton, John. *UAVs: Unmanned Aerial Vehicles.* Minneapolis, MN: ABDO Publishing, 2012.

Masters, Nancy Robinson. *Drone Pilot.* Ann Arbor, MI: Cherry Lake Publishing, 2012.

Tagliaferro, Linda. *The World's Smartest Machines.* Chicago, IL: Raintree, 2011.

Websites

DIY Drones
diydrones.com/
Check out the largest amateur UAV community on the web.

The UAV
www.theuav.com/
See pictures and read more about UAVs.

INDEX